I0816403

Words that are tricky to understand are in **bold**. Find out what they mean in the glossary.

Words that are difficult to say are in *italics*. Find out how to say them at the back of the book.

DID LIFE COME FROM THE SUN?

DISCOVER THE SCIENCE BEHIND **HELIOPHYSICS**
(hee-lee-oh-FIZZ-icks)

Written by Eliza Jeffery
Illustrated by Denis Alonso

WHAT IS HELIOPHYSICS?

Heliophysics is the study of the Sun, and how it influences Earth, outer space, and objects throughout the **solar system**, such as planets and **asteroids**. The Sun is a large **star** at the heart of our solar system. Heliophysics is considered a mix of **meteorology** and **astrophysics**.

The scientists who study the Sun are called **SOLAR PHYSICISTS.**

Throughout history, humans have looked to the Sun for answers. From ancient groups of people who tracked its movements to early scientists who studied its power, the Sun has always inspired curious minds. But could this impressive star hold the secret to life itself?

A long time ago, Earth was a very different place. There were no trees, oceans, or animals living here. Volcanoes erupted constantly, and the air was filled with **toxic gases**!

However, the Sun still shone brightly, just like it does today. The Sun's power was already at work, warming the planet and its **atmosphere**.

Scientists who study the Sun are called *solar physicists.* The Sun doesn't just provide heat and light – it also sends out different types of energy through sunlight.

This energy played an important role in Earth's early atmosphere and oceans, helping to create things called **cells**...

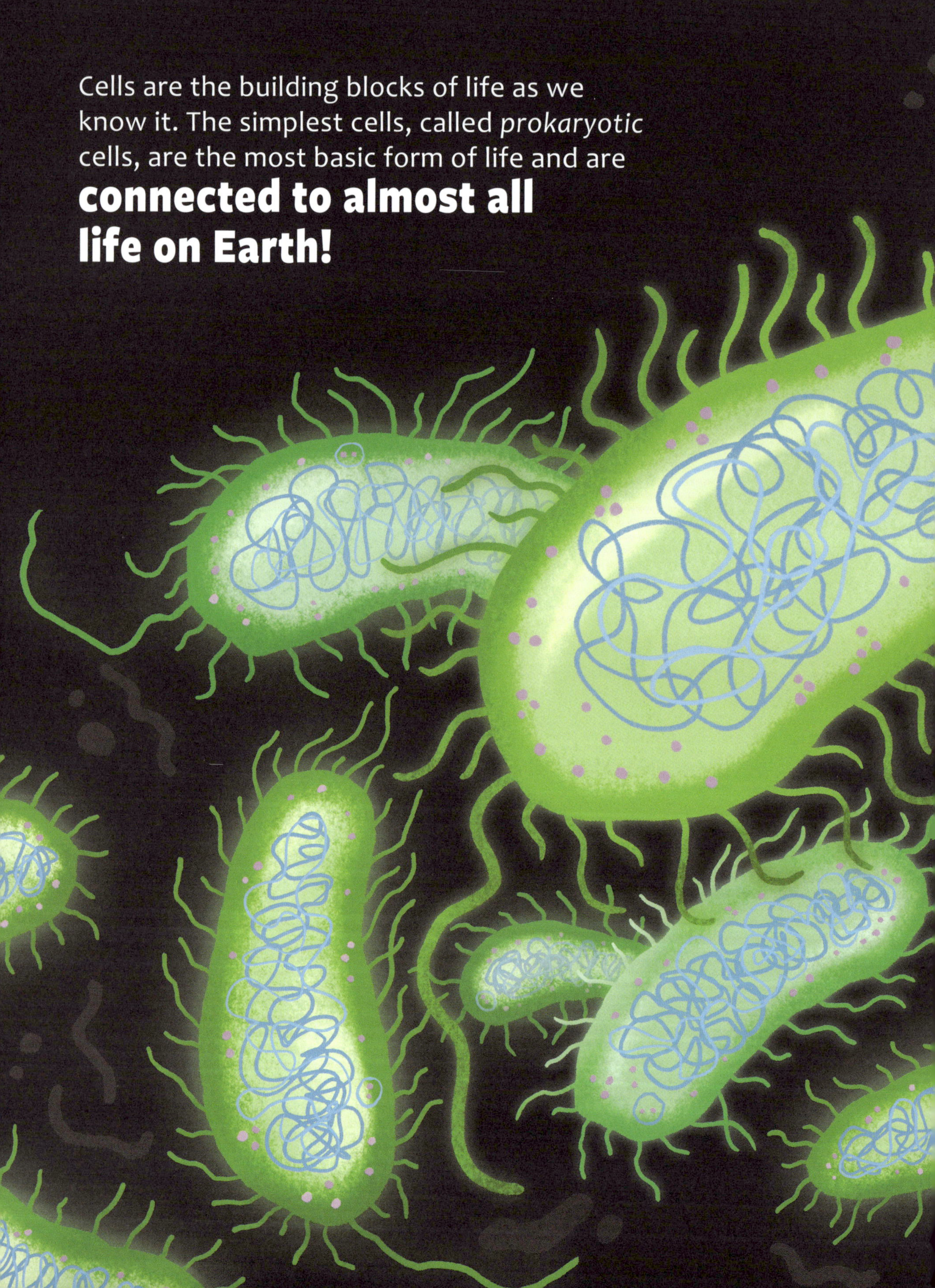

Cells are the building blocks of life as we know it. The simplest cells, called *prokaryotic* cells, are the most basic form of life and are **connected to almost all life on Earth!**

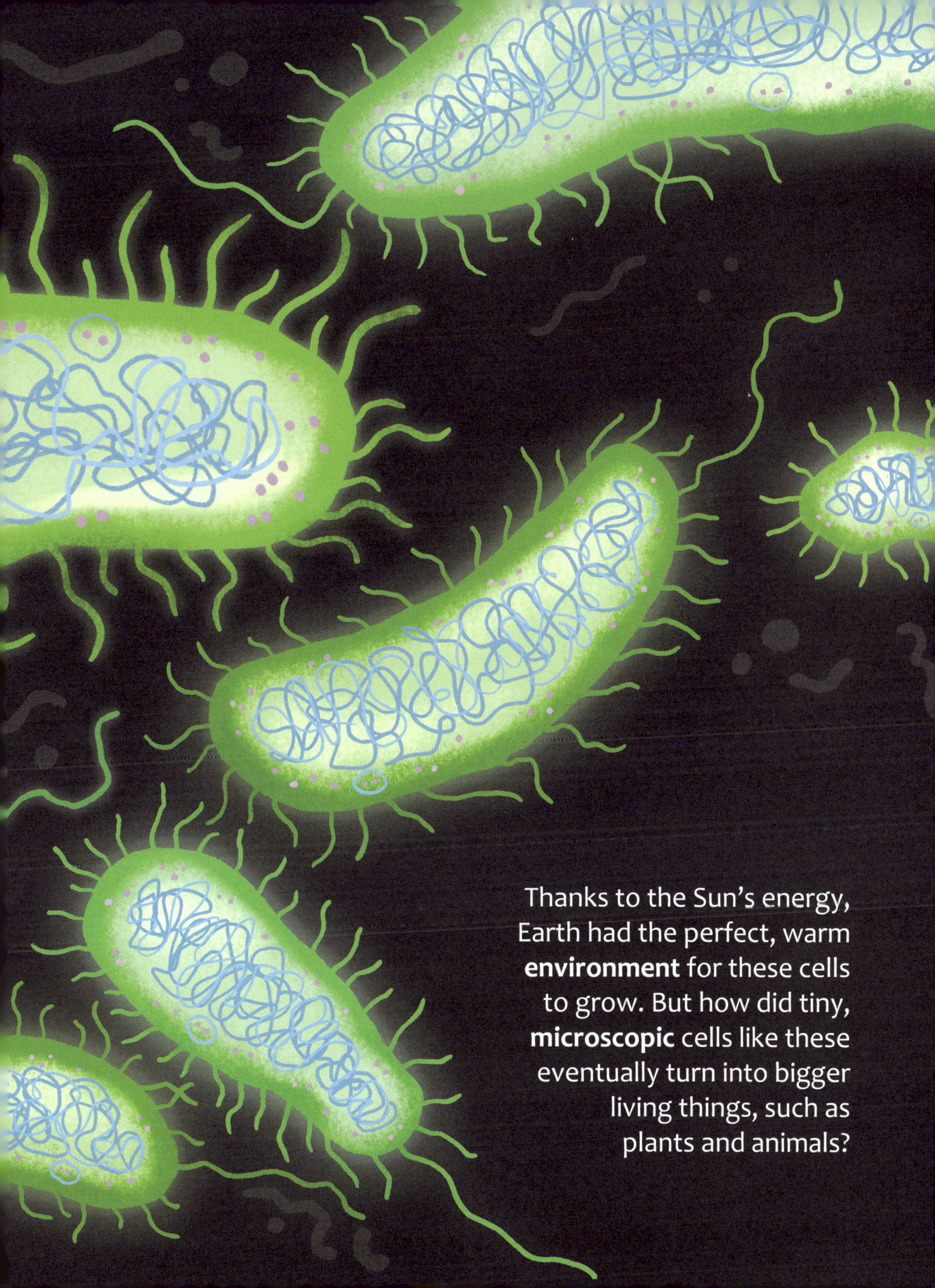

Thanks to the Sun's energy, Earth had the perfect, warm **environment** for these cells to grow. But how did tiny, **microscopic** cells like these eventually turn into bigger living things, such as plants and animals?

One big word – **photosynthesis**! Photosynthesis is where cells use the Sun's energy, along with **carbon dioxide** and water, to make food and produce **oxygen**.

Photosynthesis is like a special recipe to help cells be strong and healthy. Life would not have grown without the Sun!

With the Sun lending a hand with photosynthesis, more and more oxygen was released into the Earth's atmosphere. Oxygen is what plants and animals need to breathe!

Scientists call this the "Great Oxidation Event". It transformed the planet, making it possible for new life to grow...

This included

giant insects!

These unusual creatures ruled Earth for some time, as life began to grow in exciting and unexpected ways. But Earth hadn't finished changing yet.

Soon, Earth became home to many more forms of life. The Sun's energy made these changes possible, allowing our planet to be filled with all kinds of plants and animals!

The Sun has always been here. The same Sun we see today was shining **during the time of the dinosaurs!**

The Sun didn't just help create life – it continues to support it too! Animals, including humans, rely on plants growing for food. Without the Sun, the world as we know it today wouldn't be possible.

Humans have always been fascinated by what the Sun can do. A long time ago, people believed the Sun had healing powers and could cure sickness...

sundials were invented to tell the time by using the position of the Sun's shadow...

and today, **solar panels** are used to turn sunlight into energy for electricity. This type of energy is much better for the environment because it will never run out!

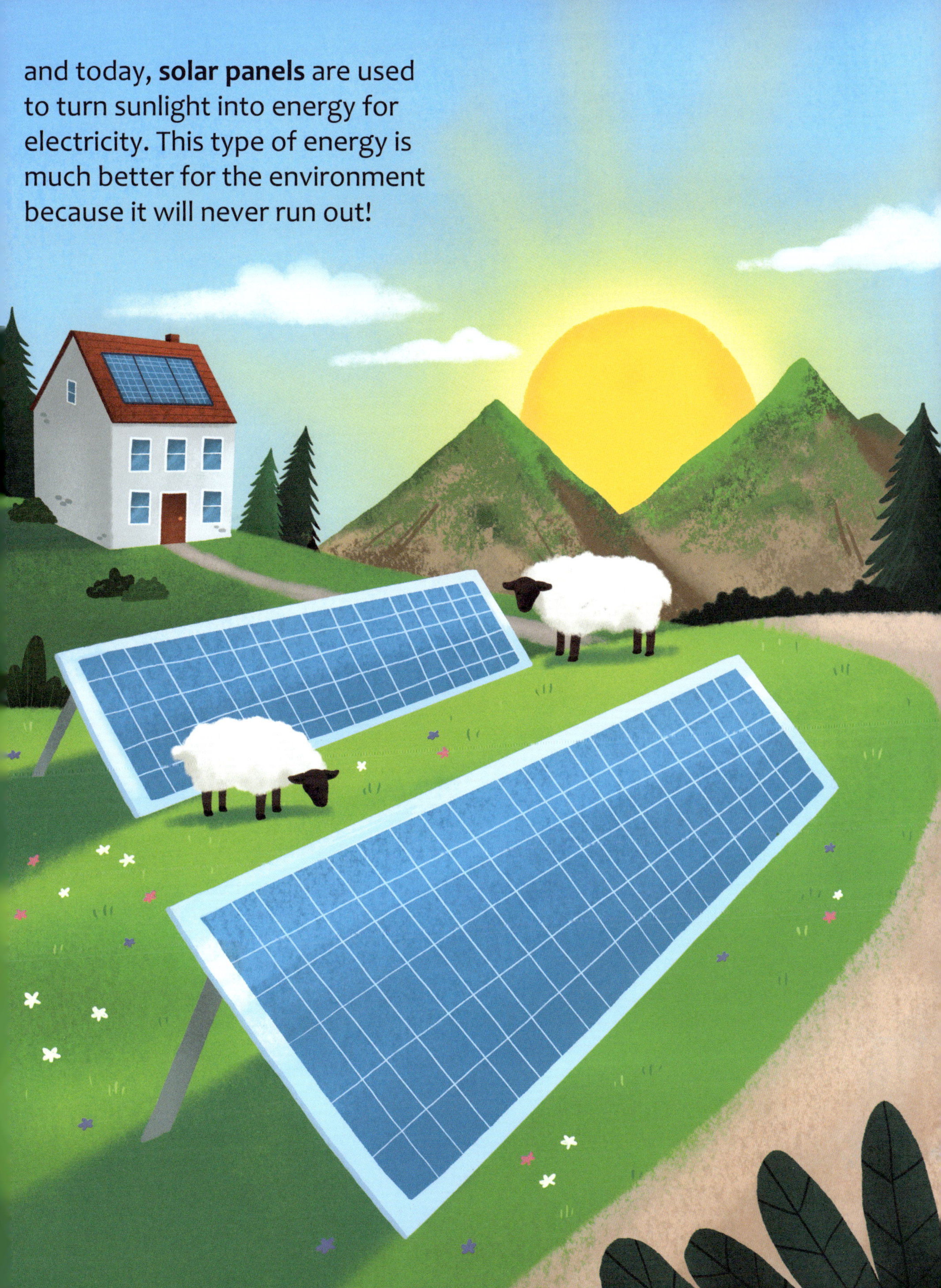

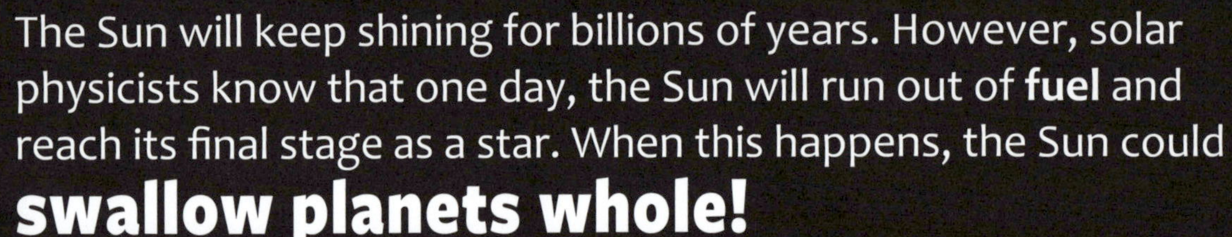

The Sun will keep shining for billions of years. However, solar physicists know that one day, the Sun will run out of **fuel** and reach its final stage as a star. When this happens, the Sun could

swallow planets whole!

But don't worry, that won't happen for billions of years – and by then, humans might be living on other planets, or even exploring distant stars!

Scientists are searching for signs of life on other planets and moons in our solar system and beyond. Could the energy of other suns have sparked life elsewhere, too? Solar physicists believe the possibilities are endless...

Science shows us that without our Sun, life would simply not exist. From the smallest cells to the enormity of space, we are all connected to the energy of this impressive star!

Types of

STARS

Our Sun is just one type of star, but there are many, many more!

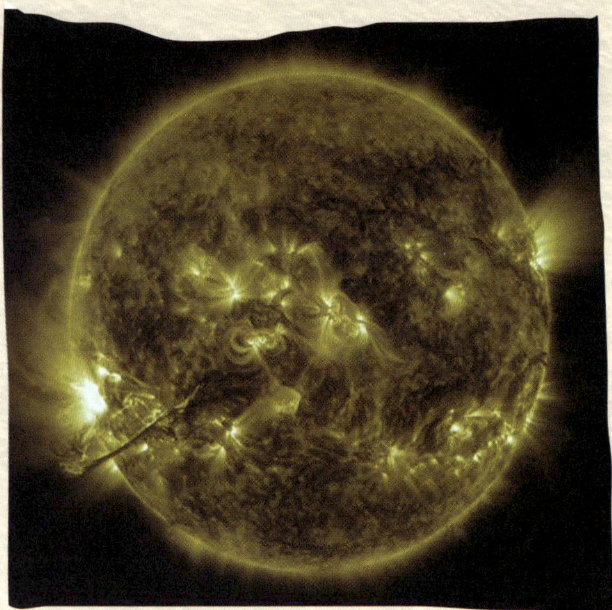

MAIN SEQUENCE STARS

Main sequence stars are stars, like our Sun, that are in the middle of their life cycle. They shine very brightly!

RED GIANTS

Red giants are stars that have grown bigger than main sequence stars. They look red because of their cooler temperature, even though they are much larger now.

WHITE DWARFS

White dwarfs are the small remains of stars that used to be bigger but have run out of fuel! They are very hot but don't shine as brightly as main sequence stars.

NEUTRON STARS

Neutron stars are the cores left behind after massive stars have exploded. They are so **dense** that a spoonful of this star weighs as much as a mountain!

RED DWARFS

Red dwarfs are small, cool stars that are the most common stars in our galaxy. They don't shine very brightly but live for trillions of years, burning their fuel slowly.

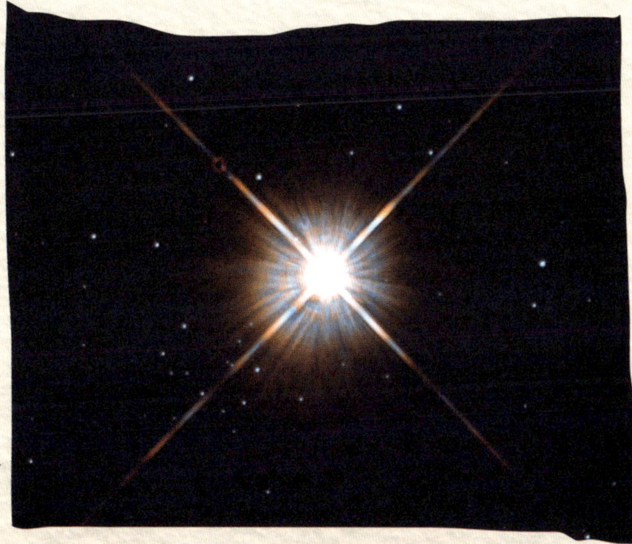

Seriously Super

SUN FACTS

Our Sun is needed for life here on Earth, but what else is there to know about this big, glowing star?

COULD WE LIVE ON THE SUN?

Unfortunately not! Although the Sun's power supports and helps create life on Earth, the Sun itself cannot support life because of its extreme temperatures!

WHAT IS A SOLAR ECLIPSE?

A solar eclipse happens when the Moon moves in front of the Sun, blocking its light for a little while. From certain places on Earth, the Moon appears to cover part or all of the Sun.

HOW OLD IS THE SUN?

The Sun is around 4.6 billion years old! It was born a long time ago from a giant cloud of gas and dust in space.

WHAT ARE SOLAR FLARES?

Solar flares are big bursts of energy and light that shoot out from the Sun's outer layers. They happen when the Sun's energy becomes too strong and bursts free all at once!

HOW BIG IS THE SUN?

The Sun is massive – it's about 1.3 million times bigger than Earth. If the Sun were a big basketball, Earth would look like a tiny marble in comparison!

GLOSSARY

Asteroids – space rocks that travel around the Sun.

Atmosphere – the gases (see right) that surround a planet.

Atoms – the smallest building blocks of matter that make up everything around us.

Astrophysics – the study of stars, planets, and everything in space. *Need help saying this? Look below!*

Carbon dioxide – an invisible gas in the air that plants take in to make food and oxygen (see right).

Cells – the smallest parts of a living thing.

Dense – tightly compacted.

Environment – everything that is around us.

Fuel – materials that are burned to produce energy.

Gases – tiny, usually invisible, particles in the air.

Meteorology – the study of weather. *Need help saying this? Look below!*

Microscopic – something that is so small it can only be seen with a microscope.

Oxygen – an invisible gas in the air that plants produce, and people and animals need to breathe.

Photosynthesis – how living things make food from sunlight, water, and carbon dioxide (see left). *Need help saying this? Look below!*

Solar panels – a panel that turns sunlight into energy for electricity or heating.

Solar system – the Sun and everything that moves around it.

Star – a bright ball of gas in the sky that gives off light and heat.

Sundial – an instrument that shows the time by the shadow cast by the Sun.

Toxic – something very dangerous.

HOW DO I SAY?

Astrophysics
a-stroh-FIZZ-icks

Heliophysics
hee-lee-oh-FIZZ-icks

Meteorology
mee-tee-uh-ROL-uh-jee

Photosynthesis
foh-toh-SIN-thuh-sis

Prokaryotic
PROH-karr-ee-ot-ick

Solar physicists
SOH-lar fizz-uh-sists

THE BIG QUESTIONS ANSWERED

This is more than just a series of books; it is a complete resource. Accompanying each book is a variety of FREE material to engage curious kids with science.

www.thebigquestionsanswered.com

Use the QR code to visit the website, download free resources, and discover other books in the series.

On the website, find out incredible things about solar physicists, including what they do, some of their greatest discoveries, and the people who have made a difference in this field of science.

The material is also available for home or classroom use, supporting all the information in this book.

Teachers' & Parents' Resources
With discussion prompts and questions, extra information, and facts around key topics.

Young Solar Physicists' Activity Pack
Fun activities for wannabe Sun experts, including creative writing, drawing, word searches, and much, much more.

The Big Questions Answered is published by Beetle Books. Beetle Books is an imprint of Hungry Tomato Ltd.

First published in 2025 by Hungry Tomato Ltd
F15, Old Bakery Studios, Blewetts Wharf, Malpas Road, Truro, Cornwall, TR1 1QH, UK.

ISBN 9781835691434

A CIP catalog record for this book is available from the British Library.

With thanks to:
Editors: Millie Burdett and Holly Thornton
Designers: Amy Harvey and Meg Holbrook
The team at Beehive Illustration
Consultant: Dr. Claire Foullon

Information in this book is up to date as of the time of writing.

Printed and bound in China.

Picture Credits:
(t = top, b = bottom, m = middle, l = left, r = right)
Shutterstock:
NASA: Chuck Carter and Gregg Hallinan/Caltech 33bl; ESA/Hubble & NASA 33mr; NASA/CXC/Univ of Toronto/M. Durant et al 33ml; NASA's Goddard Space Flight Center/Scott Wiessinger 33tr; NASA's Goddard Space Flight Center/Chris Smith (KBRwyle) 33br; NASA's Scientific Visualization Studio/SDO 32tl.